HONOR

Book 1
of the

Carbon Copy Series

C. S. Phoenix

Copyright © 2022

Ember Press

All rights reserved.

No part of this book may be reproduced in any form or by any electronic or mechanical means, including information storage and retrieval systems, without written permission from the author, except for the use of brief quotations in a book review.

Paperback ISBN **978-0-57-835071-4**

Cover Design: Chandra Watson

Book Illustration and Design: Rachel Ross

Author Photo: Marysol Onate

"… [A]n unforgettable journey. This book perfectly and poignantly dives into the truths and trials of abuse and addiction…[T]he kind of writing that cuts you open and stitches you back together again. Reflective and retrospective… Phoenix's words make one feel seen, understood, and loved…"

- **Ali Blanco, author of *If Words Could Talk***

"…[B]urns with bravery, authenticity, and heart… a bravely vulnerable poetry collection, resonant with rebirth."
- **Michael Lajoie, author of *The Summit by the Sea***

Also by C. S. Phoenix

Carbon Copy Series
Book 2 – Integrity
Book 3 - Candor

*This book is dedicated
to the younger versions of myself.
Thank you for surviving
so that we could learn to heal.
Thank you for finding a way
through all the darkness and pain,
long enough for us to become
the light we always needed.
You can rest now.*

Acknowledgements

DJ Vinatieri (The Deege), I would not be here today had you not believed in me. You saw my strength, resilience, and potential when I could only see the barriers in front of me. You gave me the courage to believe in myself and become who I was meant to be. Thank you for your friendship. Broseph, you saved my life more times than I can count, and I will be forever grateful.

To my mom. I'm an adult now, with kids of my own, and I know you did the best you could with what you had. I love you. Thank you for trusting me to share my story even though it could not be easy on you. I am glad I finally had the courage to introduce my full self to you and build our relationship better than it has ever been. You are a queen and a hero, and you will always be an inspiration to me. Also, thank you for rolling with the punches with me and helping me make this dream possible.

Rachel Ross, for sticking by my side for 20 plus years and being willing to take on this project with me. You are a visionary and have helped bring my words to life. But before that, you gave me strength and courage over and over to continue to live this life. I feel like I will never really understand why or how we get along, but I think we have one of the those loves that just doesn't need to be explained.

Sam Mobley, for offering your critique and editing so that I don't sound like a complete nimrod. I am so glad to have met you on this journey through life. Maybe one day I'll actually meet you in person.

Brenda Fowely, for giving me recording time to make this project possible on all fronts and always being happy to see me.

Mik, thank you for surviving our childhood and welcoming the story of how it looked from my perspective, as I told you in adulthood. I'm glad we have become friends and we can put those nightmarish days behind us.

Kason, thank you for existing, first off. I know you had no part in it, but without you I don't know that I would have ever been given a reason to stop running and face my demons. Also, you are a dope little brother, and I am proud of all that you have done and been through in your short time on Earth. I can't wait to see what you become!

TRIGGER WARNING

This book contains material relating to disordered eating, body dysmorphia, suicide, self-harm, and trauma. Please take care of yourself as you read.

If you are in crisis, please contact the suitable hotline for help.

National Eating Disorder Association
www.nationaleatingdisorders.org/help-support/contact-helpline
National Suicide Prevention Lifeline
(800) 273-8255
Crisis Text Line
Text HOME to 741741
National Domestic Violence Hotline
(800) 799-7233
Veterans Crisis Line
(800) 273-8255
National Sexual Assault Hotline
(800) 656-4673
Childhelp National Child Abuse Hotline
(800) 422-4453
Substance Abuse and Mental Health Services Administration National Helpline
(800) 662-4357

Shame

Shame runs deep in me
From the tip of my eyelashes
To the marrow of my bones

It started when I was four
I didn't know then
Or feel it then
But that's where the shame started

It wasn't until years later
When I found out
That what those older kids had taught me
Wasn't supposed to be taught to me
And it wasn't supposed to be done to me

And somehow
Though I didn't do the doing
I was the one who felt
Soiled

Somehow my flesh was rotten
At the touch of others
Who got to stay fresh

Shame settled in differently in later years
It wasn't just the actions of others
That brought on adulthood too fast

My body also decided
That as a nine-year-old
I should arrive into my adult form

While other little girls
Were still playing with dolls
I was getting fitted for bras
And watching my hips widen by the day

Childbearing hips
Are not featured
In Seventeen Magazine

And I was never taught better
Or different
So, I tried to starve myself away.

Shame is what I felt each time
Something wouldn't fit right
Or I only got an A, not an A+
When I didn't get first place
Or made a mistake
Each time
I was ever less than perfect

I have been trained for shame
But to this day
The most shameful thing
I've ever done
Was stay

After I said
If it's ever me or the kids, we have to leave
When you broke my belongings
And thrust your fist through our walls

After I said no and stop
Over and over
And you didn't
Stop

After you put your hands on me
And I thought
I wouldn't survive the night
I stayed

I stayed
Until you were done with me
Until you wanted something new

And that
Will always be
My greatest shame

Knowing I deserve much better than this
And accepting anything less.

Time Machine

Who are people without their trauma?
Does anyone really know?

It seems the more I learn about the world
The more I realize,
No one is untouched by trauma.
Whether it is their own,
Their parent's,
Their lover's,
Everyone's lives have been touched by trauma.

So, who were we
Supposed to be
Before this cruel world took ahold of us?

Monster

I always like to think of myself as a phoenix
I break
I burn
I'm born again

Majestic and noble

But at times
When I feel the darkness in me
I feel that I resemble more of a basilisk

Every time I feel I'm breaking
I shed my skin
And emerge
A
Larger
Deadlier
Monster

Moments

Moments are fleeting
Time is a bitch.

We have moments of joy.
Smiles on, eyes, gleaming
Then they are gone.

I have moments of pain.
So deep I can't bear to keep going
Think of the end.

But these are just moments,
Nothing more.

Life cannot be made of moments
They come and go too quickly.

Each moment,
Each memory,
Time will erase.

And we will all be left with nothing.

Look Back

I am unforgettable
And yet
So many can walk away from me
And never look back

Punishing Myself

I wasn't always efficient at hurting myself.
It took years to learn what tools worked best and for what purpose.
It started with eraser burns
In the fifth grade.
I wanted to know if I could erase myself from existence,
Instead, I learned that pain offered an escape,
And to escape was what I needed.

My favorite tools were pop tabs.
I would MacGyver that shit into a tiny blade that I could carry in the pocket of my jeans.
So, if I ever needed relief,
At school or at home,
Like MacGyver, I was ready.

By my bedside I kept a collection of broken glass.
Shards that I found lying in the street,
Someone else's bad habit to feed my own.
Each piece of glass felt a little different when it cut,
And each one left a slightly different scar.

Then there were the needles that I dug into my flesh.
By moonlight or lamp light,
Testing how much pain I could endure
By pushing a sewing needle through whatever parts of me I could grab.
Serves me right for having so much to pinch.

Taking those same needles
Adding a flame
And branding myself.
Or stealing lighters from my older brother
To just burn me like the (*B*)witch I am.

When you play with fire,
You have to play with ice
So, I poured salt on my body and held an ice cube against it
Until it sizzled through my skin.
Chemical burns,
To satisfy the nerd in me.

At some point I stole steak knives from the kitchen.
They didn't slice through my skin easily
But their serrated blade left a rough, raw edge that hurt a little more.
And healed a little slower.

It's ironic,
I got caught because I had a friend care enough about me to turn me in,
To hand me over to the people who *care* about me.
You lectured me about how I was embarrassing you
That people would think you were bad parents if they found out.
You told me to turn over everything to you.
I turned in all my tools.
You promptly returned the knives to the kitchen and the rest in the trash.
To this day, you still cut your steak with knives I used to cut my flesh.
But that really shouldn't surprise me
You like those steak knives much more than you ever liked me.

You met me halfway through my journey,
Never knowing
Or caring
What your daughter did to survive you.
I mutilated myself for four more years without you noticing.
I applied to college far away from you.
The day I realized I could escape
For real
Is the day I convinced myself,
I can be stronger than you
And to do that
I needed to stop punishing myself.

Within My Skin

At first it came as fear.
Fear of falling into my old habits.
Fear
Of not being strong enough
To stop myself
From sliding down
The slippery slope to dysfunction.

As weight melted from my frame
Compliments flooded in
I tried to explain
But no one would listen.

I want to be healthy
And this isn't good
You don't understand
My relationship with food.

But then I still wished,
That as I regained my health,
My weight would somehow,
Stay.

I was happy when the weight went up,
For a moment.
But it kept creeping
And I couldn't slow it.

I remember what my body looked like
Two months ago.
I had abs
Showing under my crop top.

And now,
Now I see loose skin
And fat that has settled itself again.

6 months ago,
Where I am now,
Was my
Hashtag goals

This is where I thought a good healthy weight would be for me.
But now,
Now I pull at my sides like I did
When I was twenty

Taking diet pills
Replacing meals with exercise
And calling it
A compromise.

I don't want to be that girl again.
I have come so far from who she was.
But I look into the mirror and cry
Because all I see, is too much of me.

Hiding In Plain Sight

I feel like I'm in junior high
Or high school again
Constantly hiding what I really am
Hoping someone will see me
Stop me
On my path to self-destruction

The only difference
Is now
I can cry out loud
I can hear my pain now

It makes me wonder
What it would have sounded like
If I was able to when I was young.

Fitspiration

The fine line between inspiration and intimidation. The line between fitsipration and why am I never enough.

Death By Dedication

What you call dedication
I call disorder.

In high school,
I was dedicated.
Dedicated to exercising in place of eating,
Dedicated to a steady regiment of diet pills and laxatives.
I looked healthy,
Because I was tearing myself apart from the inside.

In college,
I was dedicated to lunch hour swims and daily 2 hour lifting sessions,
I was dedicated to drinking more water than my body could process
And not knowing what Ben and Jerry's tasted like.

In adulthood,
I have been dedicated to sticking to the list of foods I've made
So that I don't have to obsess over my meal planning
But instead feel guilt and shame when I eat off my schedule.
I have been dedicated to my workout regiment,
Even when I am tired, injured, or ill.

What looks to the outside like dedication
Feels a lot like I'm killing myself slowly
So no one will notice.
And when I die,
In my eulogy,
They will not speak of my disorder, but my dedication

Body Checking

I learned the term body checking when I started my eating disorder recovery. I hear it and think of someone getting slammed into the glass at a hockey game. It's not so different really. Just that, instead of a large man on ice skates destroying you from the outside, it's your inner voice destroying you from the inside.

It comes in the form of always having to check your body in mirrors. Have you gained a little here or sunken a little there? Are you perfect yet? It comes from pinching and pulling at your flesh to measure if you have more give than before. Weighing yourself like you will somehow love yourself if you lost 5 pounds. Compulsively measuring your body to try to find your worth.

So, I guess it kind of does feel like a big guy on ice skates is slamming you against the glass - and that you will never feel comfortable in your own skin.

Lies

Sometimes I tell you lies
To keep you by my side.
I'm fine.
Don't worry.
I'll make it.
Just another line.

Sometimes I tell you lies
To keep you far away
I don't want you
I don't need you
Without you I'm just the same.

Sometimes I tell you lies
Just to convince myself
So my heart doesn't break
And my soul doesn't melt.

I'm a liar
I'm a thief
I'm a fraud.

Breaks My Heart

Hearing you cry
Because of me
Breaks my heart

The Road

How much longer can I fake this?
'Til they see through this smile.

Those who have always been close, are distant.
I think I need a mile.

A mile between me
And anyone I've been.

This place used to feel like home
Now the walls are closing in.

This smile can't last forever
It is fading by the day

The road is calling out to me
It is screaming out my name.

Coward

When I stand in front of an adversary
My back straightens
My chin raises slightly to the sky
I am prepared for battle.
Nothing scares me.

When someone needs protection
Comfort
My arms widen
And enclose around them in an embrace.
I, the shield to defend them.

When shelter is needed
I broaden my back
And fold into the ground
Surrounding those in need.

I am a warrior
A protector
A battlement
And a coward.

Because when I try to speak
And ask for what I need
I shrink
Wither
And I cry
Too afraid
Of being a burden
For being human

Warrior

I have realized that I have lived through too much to be loved by another.

I'm a warrior
And warriors work alone.

"What makes you say that?"

Name me a famous warrior
And their best friend

Stuck With Me

Bitch please
You look great!

I can say it to myself over and over
and never believe it.

You're rocking it!
Somehow that makes me believe.
Because I trust you.
Me, no chance in hell.
But you, I trust you.

I am here today
Because somewhere in the last 20 years,
you decided to take in this stray.

You could see that I needed help
when others would say
She can handle herself.
You fed me when I wouldn't eat.

You know that if I call
With no text preceding
Just to come over.
You will sit with me for hours
Not saying a word
Just so I don't have to be alone with myself.
Because you know that there is nothing more
dangerous to me than my own mind

You are my best friend,
And you are stuck with me,
I promise.

Too

I feel like you see me.
I have never been seen before.

It is hard for me to hear,
Reach for your potential,
Evolve,
Become more.

It doesn't make sense.
How is being more an option
When I am already too much?

Too smart,
Too loud,
Too opinionated.

Too strong,
Too athletic,
Too masculine.

Too,
Too,
Too, much.

Everyday this world tells me I need to be less.
Less to succeed.
Less to survive.

But you tell me I can be more.

17

17

A prime number

The people I know, lost to their own hand

The number of years since I have been able to hug you

The age you will forever be

17

Afterlife

When I think about you, I wish I believed in an afterlife. I wish I believed I would see you again and we could just catch up. Like you would have watched my entire life play out and we would just sit around for the rest of eternity with you giving me shit for the stupid things, consoling me for the hard times, and smiling at all the good times. I wish as we went through those memories you would be able to hold me, like I needed it then, and laugh with me, and congratulate me on all the tiny wins.

When I think about you, I wish so much that I believed in an afterlife, just so I could see you again.

Tributary

We are standing at a tributary,
    Where two paths intercede.
        Two flowing rivers,
            that have always been,
                you and me.

        There's bends and breaks
        and rocky rapids,
    pools and tiny springs.

Everything, once intertwined,
    is the beauty that life brings.

        Coming together to start anew.
        Bending and breaking as one.
        The river before us
            reflects the glorious sun.

    The breaking of dawn,
    the falling of dusk,
everything in between.

The water before us
    shimmers with life.
        Our love story told in a stream.

Scar(r)ed

It is all too fitting
Scared and scarred

For those who are not scarred are rarely scared
And those who are not scared are rarely scarred

My Table

If you won't stand next to me on a battlefield
Or walk with me through fire
You don't get to feast at my table

Love and Let Go

Loving someone and letting them go.
I feel like it's all I've ever done.

I may have loved some for wrong reasons.
I may have loved some who didn't deserve it.
But I have never,
not loved a person,
as they walk away.

Healthy Mindset

Let's talk, healthy mindset. There is a difference between, "It's all in your head and you can overcome anything if you just put your mind to it," and, "I don't have to let my circumstances determine if I'm going to keep trying."

I appreciate the people who try to motivate others to be the best and strongest version of themselves. I love that there are people who will look at you and tell you that you don't have to stay where you are or accept what has been dealt to you. However, sometimes when I hear people say you can overcome whatever you want to if you just master your mindset, I think not about the times that I have mastered my mindset, but the countless times I have not.

No one is strong all the time. Anyone who tells you otherwise is lying to you, and themselves. And when I hear people say that I just need to master my thoughts, my emotions, myself, I can't help to think about the times I've failed. The times I wasn't strong enough. The times when I almost lost my fight against the monsters that live inside of me.

Flashback Friends

For all of my friends who I love more than words can say,
I hate what we have become.

People tell me that it is part of growing up,
to lose your friends
to distance,
to time,
to change.

I want so much to have friends,
in my life,
as part of my life,
but I don't.

I have flashback friends.
People who I love to see,
to spend time with,
but have only had,
remember when,
for so long,
I'm starting to forget.

We see each other and flashback to the good old days,
but when was the last time we made a new memory?
Do you remember?

Sophie

Window open

The moon is high

Her soul begins to shake

Before dawn

Touches the sky

Her sleepy eyes do wake

She does not want to be

Of this mortal coil

At least not before noon

Why can't she sleep at night

And the day always comes too soon

She reads the cards

What her day has in store

She asked for answers

But it is the questions she truly seeks

Her crystals guard her

Guise her

Guide her

While her jams

Always beside her

Keep her company through her day

Hand me a red bull

She says

And I'll be on my way

Rachel

Do you cry?
I don't know that I've ever seen it.

You have seen me
Time and time again,
Crying.
Sad and lonely
Wondering, why?

But you have so much,
Do I call it strength?
Or are you just not pained by the things that anguish me so?
Infallible.
Indestructible.

Blue Moon

As you pressed the orange slice
Down the bottleneck
I realized,
This love will never end.

You are part of my forever.

My blue moon.

My best friend.

Unscathed

I am not one of those, self-sufficient, strong,
independent women.
I am not one of those girls that has her plans set,
knows what she wants, and is okay with being alone
as long as I am achieving my goals.
I am not smart.
I am not naturally pretty.
I am not effortless.

I am a woman who tries too hard to seem like I have it
all together,
so that you, world,
won't rip me apart.
I don't know where I am going in life.
I don't know what I'm doing.
I hope I don't starve along the way.

I wish that people would see, and understand,
it is not as easy as I make it look.
It's not that I don't cry,
but that I don't let you see me do it.
Not that I don't fear,
but that I put on the tough girl face I learn in junior
high and walk out the door in the morning.

I don't go through life unscathed
and I know, neither do you.

You Scare Me

You scare me.

You have been incredibly welcoming of all of my stories.
The silly pointless ones.
The ones that are sometimes too serious for the occasion.
You have thus far accepted all that I have put before you.
I fear it will end.
I fear I will want it to continue
and it won't.

I also fear that it will continue,
that it will deepen,
and it will be real.
I will finally have what I have wanted
and I will have to learn to live again.

Fuck You

You know
I couldn't fathom how anyone would want to say fuck you
To you

You were so readily available
Helpful
Kind

Until you weren't

And now I get it

Fuck you

March 17, 2020

I can write this on a blog that nobody reads.

My kids are the only thing keeping me alive right now.

Recordings

Some of the hardest things
For me to listen to
Are the recordings I made
When I was too sad to write
But couldn't hold in my pain
Any longer

They don't translate well
To paper
And they are far too painful
To share with the world

Army

In the year I thought I was building an army
I realized more than ever
That I have to fight my battles alone.

Beacon

And then it happens

As you are fumbling through the darkness

Just trying to make it out alive

There is a beacon of light

A soul shining

Radiant

With the same glow as your own

But brighter

Stronger

And as you draw nearer

You feel your chest rise and fall

With purpose

Your light was not extinguished as you thought

It just needed stoking

And your light is gaining strength

To burn bright

For the next lost soul

Who needs a beacon

I Have a Goal

I have a goal in life:
That my two best friends pick up the phone when I call just because they want to talk.
Not because they know that if I call without texting first it means I'm in a bad, bad place and they need to answer **no matter what**.
I want to be in such a good place
It is no longer normal to drop everything when my name shows up on the caller ID.
In such a good place that they can ask,
"How are you doing?"
Without the cautious undertone of,
"Is everything okay?"
Just because it's good to hear from me and they want to know.
That's the goal for my life.

Never Send

Here I am again
Writing letters
I'll never send.

Standards

"You either like me or you don't. It took me twenty-something years to learn to love myself, I don't have that kind of time to convince somebody else."
-Daniel Franzese

It is not your job to convince someone else of your worth, of your beauty, of your brilliance. If you learn to love yourself in all your glory and in all your flaws, your people will join you. They will find you and love you. You may not always get the love you want from them, that too, is not yours to determine.

Sometimes people will think you ask too much. Whether you are asking it of them or someone else, it doesn't really matter. What matters is where you set your standards and that you don't move them.

Do you want to be swept off your feet and whisked away to a paradise island where you can live off of coconuts and a chill ocean breeze, never parting with your true love? Great, as long as you are not willing to settle for a CPA in your hometown who's most exciting attribute is that you won't ever have to do your own taxes again. I don't care how wild your dreams are as long as you are honest about what you want, how you are going to get there, and you settle for nothing less. This is where being honest about your dreams really comes in.

I have spent too much of my life settling for someone who will give me a fraction of what I desire, because something is better than nothing. And you know what I have learned? That's BS. I would take a lifetime of being alone over being with another person that doesn't fulfill my desires.

Though I'll be honest, I don't think my desires are that out of this world. I want a home, with my family, a husband who is an active part of our family. I want us to each have our own interests but to share in them on occasion. I want us to disagree, to discuss, and to reach a compromise. I want someone who has a kind heart and doesn't just understand my giving nature but joins me in it. I want someone who tells me they are thinking about me because it will make me smile or brings me a drink because I will like it. I want a simple, humble, life, where sometimes our adventures might be climbing a mountain or sailing to Antarctica, and sometimes it will be going to the grocery store and the kids' events. I want someone who will dance like a dork with me, but also slow dance and hold me close.

I think all of this is attainable, it's not an outlandish fantasy. But it means that I can't settle for the guy who wants to Netflix and Chill, or someone who wants to keep it casual. I want someone who wants to build a life. A grand, extraordinary, common, life. And to do that I need to be steadfast in my standards, to do what I love and what makes me feel whole, and hope, that somewhere along my path I find that person and somehow overcome my Awkward AF long enough to speak to them. It doesn't mean I'll get what I want, or that they will like me back, I may not be their desire. What matters is that I never accept less than I have deemed myself worthy.

Scars

Sometimes I think I don't get to claim the things I've done
Because the proof of my actions isn't easy to see.
You see, I'm generally a pasty white color
So, the scars that I have made on myself just blend in
So, no one can see.
Well, no one but me.
There are the ones I know by heart.
I know the stories behind them,
The tool I used,
If it was just to find relief from life
Or relief in death.
I know them all too well.

Then there are the ones I only remember
When the sun kisses my skin
A bit too eagerly
And a burn reveals the difference
From one inch to the next.

There are the ones I would fixate on
Remembering the sweet taste
Of being the one to hurt myself
Before anyone else could.
The ones I have since covered with ink
As if it will somehow make me forget
That I spent years of my life
Carving into my own flesh
In order to calm my mind.

All these scars
I have
But they cannot be seen
And if they cannot be seen,
If I cannot prove the pain I put myself through
Can I even claim it happened?

I have hidden my wounds too well.

Punishing Myself, Again

When I went back to therapy, I had my standard intake.
Questions I had heard many times before.
For some reason,
I always want my therapist to think I'm doing better than I am,
Even though I'm returning to therapy.
Like I don't want them thinking that their efforts had been in vain.
It wasn't looking great going into the self-harm question,
I had already cried,
Admitted to backsliding,
Was not coping well with my false beliefs,
And then the question,
"Do you ever intentionally injure yourself?"
I responded with a proud, beaming smile,
"I have not cut myself since February 18, 2005!"
This was an accomplishment I was truly proud of.
"That's great! What about scratching, biting, or hitting yourself?"
I justified,
"I mean, sure, I have nervous ticks.
I scratch the back of my thumbs when I'm anxious

And I've bitten myself here and there.
Nothing major."
Then I look down at my legs
Black and blue.
It looked like someone had used my thighs for a punching bag.
Then I remembered,
Three days prior,
When I had used my legs for a punching bag.
I realized,
I had been so focused on not picking up a blade or broken glass again,
I had moved on
To only using myself
As a weapon against me.

Another Day

I used to think it was just another day
Just another hug

It's how he greeted me everyday

Now I look back and think
Maybe he was saying goodbye

I don't know if that makes me happy
Because I was worth saying goodbye to

Or sad because he knew he was leaving me behind
And didn't bother to tell me.

Target Practice

I never knew why
You hated me so much.
I kept to myself
And didn't bother you.
I just wanted to succeed
So my parents would see me.
Somehow,
That made me a target.

I still wear the scar
Of the day
I ran from you
Throwing rocks at me.
It wasn't the first time I felt like an animal
But it was hard not to feel like a treed coon.
I tried to climb high enough
To get out of range
To use the branches as extra protection.
Somehow falling from a 50-foot evergreen
Was less scary than you.

I was just a little girl.
I don't even remember your name.

Goodbye

You were so happy the last time I saw you.
I'm starting to wonder if you knew that would be our last hug,
So, you made it extra-long and extra tight.
I wonder what I would have done if I were in the room with you that night.

I've always understood why you needed to leave.
I would like to think that I would still let you find your solace in death.
But only after I got to say goodbye.

Alternate Endings Part I

Take me to that alternate timeline
Where my best friend didn't kill himself when I was 15.

I always wonder,
Would I have survived this long?
Or would I have been the cautionary tale,
The reason other people stayed alive?
God knows the pain from losing him
Kept me alive.
Knowing what it felt like on the other side,
I couldn't do that to anyone.
I even vowed,
As long as there was the possibility
Of one person being hurt,
I had to continue to suffer through my pain.

Maybe though
It would have been a happy ending.

Life's a Chore

Man, this is amazing
Have you heard this song?
You won't believe what happened at work
Dinner's almost done

I read and interesting article
The sunset caught my eye
I hit a new PR today
I swear I'm lifting more than a guy

As I speak
My smile fades
The joy seeps from my eyes
I'm talking to an empty room
As I have for most my life

Life is joyous
Sure, it's true
There is so much to explore
And yet
Having no one to share joy with
Makes life a painful chore.

Handgun Lobotomy

I keep daydreaming
Of a handgun lobotomy

An easy end
To the pain I can't seem to shake.

I know I won't.
I can't.
I already feel the guilt.

I can't feel your love for me now,
But I can feel your anguish if I go.

If I could just get a few moments of silence
I think I could figure out how to get through this.

If it could be temporary
I would pull the trigger.

Spiteful

I never found out who
Wanted me to die.
They never signed their name
To the notes they left in my locker.

Lucky for me
I was a spiteful child.
All they did was convince me
To hold on through the pain.

Bad influence

I was a straight "A" student
"A" team athlete
Student council officer
Community service volunteer
Straight edge kid
And apparently a bad influence

My friend's parents
Didn't want me around their children
Because they thought
I would rub off on them
As if trauma and depression
were contagious

They thought I hurt myself for fun
That it was a hobby of mine
To want to die
They thought I would convince
Their precious babes
To follow me into my darkness

A bad influence
Only caring
What trouble I could be for them
No one thought
That maybe
I just needed a friend

Worry

Sometimes, my friends question my sanity because they disappear, in a normal, taking their own time and space, kind of way, and I worry. Sometimes, they don't post anything on socials after posting regularly or don't show up to the gym for a couple days and I call them incessantly, asking them if everything is okay.

They tell me I am such a mom because I'm always worried that they have, well, died.

They make jokes about me being overprotective. They think I need to calm down and chill out a little. But I don't know if I have that in me because I've overlooked people's pain before.

I have hugged friends with beaming smiles and never seen them alive again. I worry, because I know when I am presenting a strong, happy front to the world and start disappearing, it's because I don't plan on being around much longer.

So, I would rather be the friend that worries too much and calls, than the friend who thinks everything is okay and regrets never seeing her loved ones again.

Land Speed

If my legs raced
As fast as my thoughts

I would break the fucking land speed record.

Allow

I allow myself one bowl of cereal each Sunday morning.

I
Allow
Myself
One bowl of cereal each week.

I don't actively
Calculate
It into my day
But I also don't eat it until I'm so hungry I can't stand it anymore.

I know it's just cereal
And I know I allow it
And I know it's still not perfect
Or healthy
But at least I allow it now.

Before,
I would just stay hungry.

F-I-N-E

I imagine going through pictures
And coming across any of those ones
Where I look
F-I-N-E
Fine
And getting that motivational speech
That always seems to follow,
"With dedication and willpower,
You could look like that again."

I try to hold it together
Take the comments in stride
Remember,
They don't know any better.
They say,
"You could be like that again."

I don't want to be like that again!
What am I 20 in that picture?
That means I've been starving myself for 10 years
I've been addicted to diet pills for 5
I often think about taking a knife to my own flesh
And just cutting all the excess off.
I don't remember what it was like to enjoy a meal.
But I was skinny.

I want to be able to look at myself in mirror
Without finding every imperfection.
Without buying clothes
And never having the confidence to put them on.
I want to look at food as delicious sustenance
Not caloric intake.
I want to enjoy being naked in front of a lover
Being intertwined
Without wondering if I fold too much in places that I don't deem perfect.

I know I could lose weight and look like that again.
For fuck's sake,
I've done it three times in the last year.
Never on purpose.
Each time
Desperately trying to hold on to my health.
Each time
Watching it slip through my fingers
As if I didn't have a choice.
And as I slipped away
Into smaller pants sizes
People became so vocal
"Wow, you look great!"

"Help me!"
I scream
"I haven't eaten in days.
I'm so hungry,
But if I eat, I get nauseous.
I'm dropping pounds by the day.
I need support.
I need guidance.
I need someone to listen!"

"That's nice, honey.
Keep up the good work."

Nobody cares
Because I'm skinny again.
And skinny is all
Anyone wants me to be.

Not Finished Yet

When the world gets heavy
Press it
Pull it
Squat it

When the weight on your shoulders seems too much
Brace your core
Press through the ground
And stand that shit up

When your legs are tired
And you feel like you can't go on
Take one more jump
One more stride
One more step

You're not finished yet

Patience

What I want right now
Is to feel good in my body
And to lose weight
And to eat cake
And to get strong
And to get rest
And to move mountains.

And by now
I mean like NOW

I think I need a dose of patience.

Repeating It

I am strong
I am beautiful
If I keep repeating it
I'll believe it

If this body would just look like the girls
You know the ones
Guys look at like they are candy

I am strong
I am beautiful
If I keep repeating it
I'll believe it

If I could just lose this last bit of fat
Get down to 18 percent
Not this 20 I'm sitting at

I am strong
I am beautiful
If I keep repeating it
I'll believe it

If this skin would just tighten
Be supple and firm
Like I assume it was when I was young

I am strong
I am beautiful
If I keep repeating it
I'll believe it

I don't know
I would never look at my body then
I was too ashamed of it

I am strong
I am beautiful
If I keep repeating it
I'll believe it

I've been fighting myself
Pinching and pulling
Never accepting for so long

I am strong
I am beautiful
If I keep repeating it
I'll believe it

If I keep repeating it
I'll believe it

If I keep repeating it
If I keep repeating it
If I keep repeating it

Sickness of the Mind

You see eating disorders
Aren't a disease of the body
They are a disease of the mind.
I can nourish my body all day long.
Balance my eating and my exercise
Train with intention
Be "healthy"
But as long as I still have to fight back thoughts
Like,
"I need to stop eating"
"What did I do to deserve this snack?"
"Maybe, if I don't feed my hunger, just let my stomach growl for a while, I'll lose that weight."
"Why can't I be smaller?"
"I wish I didn't have this squish."
"Disgusting."

As long as that stays true
I know I am still sick.
Proud,
That I don't let it hurt my body
But still sick.
Because it isn't a sickness of the body
It is a sickness of the mind.

Better

I wish better meant
Better,
Not just,
Not as bad as before

I'm not weighing myself daily
Or measuring my body fat.
Seeing if my waist is getting any smaller
Or looking at old pictures to compare the shape of my face.

But I still pinch at the extra skin
That folds over when I'm sitting.
I still walk past every mirror
To see how apparent my flaws are.
I still contemplate too much
If I've really earned something sweet.
I still try to convince myself
That I chew gum for any other reason than to convince myself not to eat.

But I also focus on my training
And get stronger each week.
I eat food when I'm hungry
And don't always cry afterward.

So, I'm better than I was before.
But better
Doesn't mean
Better.
And I still struggle
Everyday.

More Cushion for the Pushin'

I just want someone to think I'm pretty without a follow-up of, I like thick women, or more cushion for the pushing.

I weighed myself. I'm 200 point something, but either way, over 200 again. And I cried and cried. I'm trying to trust my body. I'm trying to listen but when I do, I just gain weight. I want to eat popcorn at our movie night, but I don't feel like I deserve popcorn.

I'm sick of skinny, small girls posting about body positivity when they will never understand that even with their bell rolls and pushed out stomachs, the world will always look at me as the big girl, even if I don't have belly rolls and my stomach doesn't stick out. I'm always the one in the wrong because of how I am. Because my body is what it is. I try to find peace in her. I try to find strength and empowerment. I try to find purpose.

During this, I just kept hearing in my head, "No one will love you like this. Why would anyone want to be with someone who looks like you?" And it all comes down to that, to be loved, you must be small, and I want to be loved, so I have to be small. But I'm, I'm not small, so it must mean I can never be loved. And I just want to be loved.

But my boys tell me they love me. They tell me I'm the best. They even tell me that I'm beautiful. But it isn't enough. They don't really know me. Or maybe they know me better than anyone. They have known me their wholes lives. I wish them loving me was enough.

I talked to them about what's wrong, because they came to hug me and make things better. It didn't work. But we talked about loving our bodies, because we all have our own, unique bodies and skills. And that I want them to love their bodies and themselves. They need to start now, **because trying to learn to love yourself and body after you have hated it for so long is really hard.**

I want to run, and run, until I can't move anymore. That's how I feel right now. And I hate running.

I was feeling a bit better. Had a crying hangover but was getting going. Then my mom asked if I was going to need help with football (as if I haven't managed my entire life putting on a face for others without anyone noticing). I told her I was good. I was getting myself breakfast and she asked if I needed anything from the store, to put it on the list, and if there is anything I need, she'll do whatever it takes to get me back on track.

I felt so helpless and pitiful. I don't know how to explain it. Just that the idea of someone wanting to help me be better makes me feel more broken. Weak and helpless is not my style. But maybe it's that I only know how to deal with things on my own. I know how to get myself out of a funk or snap out of it. I don't know how to do it with an audience, because I've never had people notice before.

Rather Be Skinny

I tell myself I would rather be fat and love myself
But the truth is
I would rather be skinny

Healing and Hurting

When healing and hurting take place in the same moment it is hard to know what to feel. I look at my body, with a few extra pounds on it. I'm disappointed but not disgusted. I say thank you to my body for letting me learn to trust it. Knowing that on the other side of this we can find peace and health. But I also am feeling more insecure about my body again. I don't want to see it in a mirror. I don't want to feel it folding over on itself. But I want to love it, no matter what it looks like. Like so many other things, I must go through this hard, painful part, to find the other side.

Fix Me

I love when people try to fix me.
I just don't like that I feel more broken afterward.

Intoxicating

There is nothing more intoxicating
Then a will to live

Drug

I think I realized
Why it's so hard
For me
To let you go

You have been my dopamine hit
My antidepressants
My drug to keep me going
When I don't have enough within myself

I'm afraid
Without you
I will lose my grip
On what light I've found
And I don't want to be in the dark anymore

Pressure

It makes me sad
That we don't talk
Like we used to

But we are not
A wound
So I will not
Put pressure on us

Alternate Endings Part II

Maybe
We would live in a little mountain town
Foster and adopt kids
Who just needed love.
More love than they thought they deserved.

We would play punk rock
And emo music,
But never forget about the classics either.

We would let the kids cry when they needed to,
Because we never got to.
But we would also teach them to be brave in the face of adversity,
Because life never stops being hard.

We would pour our hearts
Into other humans
Until the world was filled with people
Who understood,
We all deserve love.

Maybe
We would move to the city
You would be a bartender
And hold the secrets of strangers
Tight, because they need someone they can trust.

I would work at a youth center
And help underserved kids
Find their path in life

Your girlfriend would be an artist.
Respected in her field
But just wild enough to keep your attention.
My boyfriend would run a farm-to-table restaurant
He would be down-to-earth
And ride a motorcycle.

They would sometimes question our closeness
And we'd have to have jealousy talks,
A lot, in the beginning.
But they would come to realize
That love
Is not always romantic
And so, a mutual love would grow between us all

As we transition through life sharing a loft
And eventually moving on to live apart from each other.
We would cherish the time we had
And the growing up we did together.

Maybe
We would backpack across Europe
Fall in love with a little town
And never leave.

Maybe
You would be a teacher
In our hometown
And continue to impact those around you
Everyday.

Maybe
We would stay friends forever.

Maybe
We would drift apart.

But all I have is
Maybe
Because I lost you
Too young.

Take me to that alternate ending
Where my best friend didn't kill himself when I was 15.

I Can Handle Death

I can handle death
Better than moving on.
At least in death
It is final.
You will always be missing that part of your life.

When someone moves on from you,
You still have to see their face in a crowd
And know you are strangers again.

Hollow

For the first time
In a long time
I didn't feel alone
I felt like a had someone in my corner
And now that corner is empty

Maybe there was too much pressure
To fill my emptiness
Even though I told you
It wasn't your responsibility

Now that emptiness feels
Hollow
Dark
Daunting

Weakest Link

Sometimes I think
The easiest way to end this cycle
Of depression and abuse
Is to end the chain

If I didn't have kids,
The easiest way to end this cycle
Would be to break it
Remove myself
And hope the circle breaks entirely.

Maybe, only being as strong as the weakest link
Isn't such a bad thing.

Warrior's Heart

Sometimes a warrior needs to rest
To sit by the fire
Lay down his sword and shield
And remember
Why he fights

Without purpose
He is but a war machine
Blades and blood
Death bringer

To fight to the death
You must know
What you wish to live for

How

I know why people are complicated, I want to know how.

People are complicated because we are all individual organic computers perpetually taking in an infinite number of variables, processing, and trying to make sense of them.

We are complicated because we are given thousands of questions with no answers and expected to figure it out.

We are complicated because things that feel right don't make sense and things that make sense don't feel right.

We are complicated because we mean what we say but we don't say what we mean and everyone else is the same, so in our search for answers we only find more questions and confusion.

I know why people are complicated.

I want to know how.

How do you grieve your losses?
How do you celebrate your successes?
How do you manage the in between?
How do you smile when you are happy, when you are nervous, when you are mischievous?
How do you cry when you are sad, mad, hurt?
How do you heal?
How do you survive?
How do you thrive?

I know why people are complicated.
I want to know how.

Grief is Tricky

I have been grieving our friendship.
Not because we aren't friends,
But because we aren't friends like we used to be.

But today I realized,
It is not the friendship I grieve,
It is who I was able to be in our friendship.

I was able to be me.
Unapologetically, me.
And since,
I have not found a safe place to do so.

Walk Away

Stay single until you meet a person who wants you
Not your body
Not your status
Not your energy
But YOU
The shiny and the dull parts
The happy and the sad parts
The strong and the weak parts
The classy and the rachet parts

If they are given a multiple-choice question about
what they love about you and don't choose
All of the Above
Walk away
Trust me

Peachy Keen

When people ask me,
"How are you?"
I respond by saying,
"Peachy."

It's not that my life is peachy keen
Or that I'm always optimistic.
It's because no one wants to hear,
"It's been a rough go, but I'm still trying."
Or,
"I barely got out of bed today."
Trust me, I've tried those,
They say, "That's nice," and walk on.
Because they don't ask to know
They ask out of polite compulsion.
I say, "Peachy,"
Because it is a non-answer
To the non-question people ask.

When I ask, "How are you doing?"
I genuinely want to know.
And when you reply, "Peachy."
I don't believe you.

Safety

Safety is gravely overlooked. Especially, the feeling of safety derived from others. Safety you don't have to fight for. Because safety you have to fight for is just fear and living in fear may keep you safe, but it doesn't feel like safety.

We are social creatures, whether we like it or not. We are pack animals. We are not made to weather the storms alone, but many of us do. Many of us don't know any other way to remain safe, because it's those who were supposed to protect us that hurt us. So, when comfort and safety are given, we reject it out of fear.

We may have people in our lives that would be there for us if we ask. We may have people who stand up for us when we are not around. We may have people who make our lives safer. That does not always mean we feel safe. Some people bring the feeling of safety and security with them and that feeling matters. Feeling safe gives us the opportunity to relax and let down our guard. Unfortunately, the people who feel safe don't always have your safety in mind, and they hurt you. Unintentionally. Then we learn that fear keeps us safe better than comfort. But we still long for comfort.

Every warrior wants to be able to lay down their sword from time to time.

Afraid to Feel

I'm working on healing
But I'm afraid
To feel

It's been so long
Since I knew how

I'm afraid
If I learn
To feel
Again

Everything I have kept at bay
Will come crashing down my door
Every night I convinced myself I was fine
Every time I survived

Numbing kept me going
And I want to keep going
But I want to do more than survive

I know if I want to feel the ups of life
I must feel the downs
And there are less downs than ups these days
So maybe now is the time
To learn to feel
So, if the world crashes down again
I'll be ready this time

Healing From Survival

I have c-PTSD, that basically means my trauma has been ongoing. That my trauma compounded on other trauma, leaving behind very little, normal brain, to return to. We've all heard of the chicken and the egg, never knowing which came first. My story is similar – I don't know if the abusive nature of my father made me an easy target for my neighbor or if being molested made me an easy target for my dad.

What I do know, is that I developed coping skills and resiliency to survive whatever life threw at me. A big one was **independence**. I can do anything myself. Another was **indifference**. I can survive without people, love, attention, affection. Things, that I have since realized, make life livable. I developed the ability to blend in, like a zebra in a herd, so no one could single me out. One of the ways I did that was by being skinny enough, pretty enough, and smart enough to seem just like anyone else. But there was a catch.

I was skinny enough because I needed to **control** something in my life. I couldn't control how I was treated by my family, or who touched my body, or if anyone would be my friend – but I could control if I was eating. And when I controlled what I was eating, I almost felt normal. I found my solution. I had control.

Until my control, took control of me.

I have spent so long surviving; I didn't know any other way to be. Trying to control the world around me so that I felt safe has taken a toll. I am too exhausted to live, which makes surviving seem meaningless at this point. But I didn't fight this hard to let survival kill me, so I need to find a new way. Surviving has started to take away my life, and I want to live, so I must figure out how to heal from the things that have kept me alive. I think it will take a good bit of gratitude and grace.

Pound Puppy

They say dogs resemble their owners.

We got her when she was 3
They said they didn't know her history
But could tell she had been through a lot.

In her young age
She had been used.
Her body
Bred
For someone else's benefit

She is incredibly loving
But when she is scared
She gets mean

A trainer said she is not aggressive
Just very anxious around other dogs
She just needs to feel safe
And she will let her personality shine

She is athletic and playful
And she thinks the best of everyone
She loves to cuddle
And trusts people more times than they deserve.

I mean,
They do say dogs resemble their owners
But let's face it
She is me.

Smile

Give it time
I always get my smile back.

The Myth of the Mermaid

Oft I wonder
If this is why
I don't have many friends
Or romantic suitors.

They always ask questions
That make me feel like I'm
Drowning
In shallow nothingness.

So, I grab their hands
And ask them to swim deeper.
They start to faulter
So, I pull them with me
To the depths.

They either escape
And spread tales
Of the sea monster
Who looked like beauty.
Or they drown
Trying to be what I need.
But I guess
They can't breathe down here.

My Style

Beaming bright smile
Hiding
Sad
Lifeless eyes

Wit and humor
Building a façade
Of confidence

Too Much to Drink

I'd like to normalize thanking people when they help you. Especially when they don't know they are helping you.

Last night I drank - a lot. What other people view as just a good time left me thinking, "I need to be sober." I got too close to the edge I have spent my whole life avoiding. I felt numb. And it was glorious. It was refreshing and that is dangerous.

I knew I was crying, but I didn't have to feel any of the pain or fear that caused the tears. I just got to float away in the buzz of not having to be me for a short time.

I have spent my life teetering between two ledges. The first, letting go of it all, with no hope for a new day. I have wanted to die longer than some of my friends have been alive. Most of my life I have wanted to be rid of the burden of life. But I can't, because I always put other people before myself, and that would hurt someone. I am built to carry pain, not cause it.

The second, diving into the things that stop life, temporarily. Starve myself until I blackout. Take enough pills that I don't feel things. Exercise enough that adrenaline is the only feeling that exists. And now, drinking so much alcohol that all my problems just went away. I've always seen the draw of it all, of addiction. Who wouldn't want to leave behind reality for a fuzzy low hum of nothingness? But I have put in too much work to give up now. I don't want to chase those glorious fuzzy numb feelings. I want to feel.

I guess I'm just going to be a lot less fun now.

Wonder

My whole life people have given me odd looks
Because I spend too much time wondering.

Wondering what could be achieved
If we all believed.
In something.

I may never stop getting sideways glances
From the automatic masses
But I will never stop wondering
What the world would be
If everyone would just
Wonder
A little bit more.

Envy

The envy I felt
For all the girls
Who felt comfortable in their skin

Who didn't have a six pack
But loved themselves anyway

The ones who didn't obsess
Or even question what they ate

I hated you so much
Because I had run out of room to hate myself
So I had to extend my hate
Onto you

I didn't hate you out loud
Or to your face
Just inside of me

I recognize now
That hate
Was just pain

I've healed that pain now
And I don't hate you
Or envy you

In fact
I am proud of you
For loving yourself
Much longer
Than I have been able

Tides of Life

We ebb and flow
Through heartbreak and love
Hurt and healing
Pleasure and pain

We must swim through
The tides of life

Time Flies

Oh,
How a week can change things

A day,
Even a moment.

Yesterday,
Felt so different.

Being You

You don't know
How many times
You have
Saved my life
Just by
Being You.

Walks

I like to go for walks
Because it gives me a chance
To smile at strangers.

Tattoos

I used to not get tattoos
Because I was afraid of placement.
I could never find a place on my body that I was not
afraid would grow
Or shrink
Or distort over time.

I felt like I didn't deserve
To host art on my body
If my body was not a canvas
People wanted to
Gaze upon.

Turning Point

I was asked yesterday, "When was the last time you just ate something because you wanted to?"
I just shook my head and cried.
Don't get me wrong. I know I have. I know it. But I can't remember when. I can't remember a time when I ate something without wondering if I deserved it, or how it would affect my daily intake. What kind of exercise I would need to do to make up for said food. If I would become fat by eating one thing once or fear that I would binge on it, or worse, dive back into obsessively restricting. Every time I ate food, my thoughts would rage. Eating caused more stress than it was worth. To the point that a friend asked me this question and all I could do was cry and shake my head because don't remember the last time I wasn't afraid of food.

The Stories We Tell Ourselves

It's funny the stories we tell ourselves. I told myself that I had this bottle of MiraLAX because sometimes I eat things I'm allergic to and it just happens to help me not bloat too much after. I've told myself a lot of things over the years to make me feel like I didn't have a problem.

So, to the people who are hearing my story for the first time, after knowing me for years. You know why you didn't know I was struggling? Because I didn't let you. How could I let you know if I couldn't even admit it myself?

What other stories have I told myself?

Trying to Love You

I'm trying to love you.

I promise you,
I am.

It just gets hard sometimes.
I have hated you for so long,
Love feels,
Uncomfortable.
But,
I am,
Trying
To love you.

Pinch Me

I have been accepting my body lately.
Loving it, even.
And tonight, as I sit down
I see the little bit of fat that sits at my side,
I pinched it.
There really isn't much there.

But memories flood back
Of each time you pinched me
And told me I need to fix this.
Asking why I wasn't as small as the other girls
Or just telling me that I was a disappointment.
Afterall, who would want to love someone
With fat you could pinch.

And I realized,
All these years,
Measuring my worth
Inversely to the amount
I could pinch at my side
Was only how *you* taught me
To measure my worth

And that pisses me the fuck off.

Because I am worth of so much more than that,
Whether or not you can pinch the fat on my side.

Rock In My Shoe

Do you ever get that feeling
Like you don't know what to do?
When on sunny days,
It's raining.
And in all the joy around you,
You somehow still feel blue?

There's just this aching feeling
Each time I move I feel it more.
It's a stabbing feeling
Every time my foot hits the floor.
I just can't shake it.
I don't know what to do.
It's like I'm running in circles
And I've got a rock in my shoe.

With each step I get more restless.
But I can't just sit and stew.
I have to somehow keep moving
But I've got a rock in my shoe.

It rattles around inside there
Like the thoughts inside my head.
It's a punching aching pain
Like the harsh words you've always said.

It hurts my toes,
It hurts my heel,
It even hurts my heart
Because I know if I don't stop hurting,
I will soon, sure fall apart.

The fear of never making it to where I want to be
Of dreams within that will never make it to reality.

This pain,
This pain,
This aching pain,
Just make it go away!

My laces tight,
I can't undo
And it's only now that I start to feel the rock within my shoe.

I walk on and on ignoring pain
But I think I'm finally through.

With one swift pull,
The lace comes out,
And my deed is nearly done.
Through the clouds I vaguely see the shining of the sun.

The grass is green,
The air is warm,
My toes kiss morning dew.

Oh, how good it feels to know,
You were only a pebble in my shoe.

I'm running barefoot, now, awhile,
To see what I can see.

I keep my sneakers close at hand,
A sandal here or there,
But now, I just like the feel
Of my feet when they are bare.

I Sleep

I sleep
More often than not
These days.

There are still
Nightmares
And night terrors
Once in a while.
They make for rough days.
But mostly,
I sleep.

Blocked

I thought I had him blocked everywhere
I destroyed myself for decades
Just so he would be proud of me

I apparently missed one
And he found me
Followed me

"That's my girl"
"She's amazing"
Delete
Block

Sigh of relief

You don't get to take credit
You don't get to claim me
I worked for this
For me

No Need to Hide

I was always magic
I was always fire
I was always fury

I don't need to hide it anymore

wild

I'm wild
I know

Not a
Get drunk
Party hard
Whoo girl
Kind of wild

A take a bite out a of a still beating heart
A run barefoot through the woods
A carnal connections under the moonlight
A bleed for me and I will bleed for you
Kind of wild

But I usually just say
"I'm not everybody's cup of tea."

Me

I traveled the world
Looking for a place to belong
And found nothing.

There was not one place I could fit.
I wept as loneliness fell over me,
Stared at myself in a mirror
And locked eyes with the monster inside of me.

He spoke of things
Of which I did not agree.
Weakness and hate
Which I knew were not my own.

My tears dried,
A smile crept across my face,
And I realized
I don't belong anywhere
Because I am everywhere.

I am mystic
Enchanted
And magical

I am what no one else could ever be.

Me.

Love

I want a love that defies gravity.

Passion.
Fearless action.
Adventure.
Knowledge.
Wisdom.

I want to float.
To feel like there is nothing that can bring me down.

This,
Is how I want to love me.

I May Be Broken

I may be broken.
Shattered.
Torn.
Destroyed.

I have seams that will never mend.
Scars that will never heal.

I may be broken.
But I am beautiful.

Broken Beauty

I used to think that being broken took my beauty away. I felt like everyone could see that I was dirty and used. I felt like there was a sign on my back that announced to the world that my worth was gone.

What I've learned through everything in my life is that you can be broken and you can be beautiful at the same time. That quite possibly, being broken enhances your beauty, while the light shining through all of your cracks exposes how fantastic you truly are.

I Disassembled My Monster Today

As I cried, not able to figure out why I was letting myself tumble backwards into my favorite dangerous pastimes of risky behavior and self-destruction. The monster that I have been fighting for as long as I can remember grew and lorded over me. My fear and sadness began to sink in. Then a kind voice told me to look at the monster and tell her what I saw. I turned toward this dark beast looming over me and I looked at it. And when I looked right at it, I did not see a devilish grin, or jaws full of teeth that could rip me limb from limb, I saw images of me at various ages. I saw them screaming, crying, fighting, or being trapped in silence. It was not fair. They had already lived through that. Why was it happening again? I had to do something. So, I dove, chest deep into the shadow, wrapped my arms around her tiny waist and pulled.

I placed her on the ground to find it was me at five years old, dressed in jean shorts with the bottoms rolled up, a t-shirt that was once perfectly tucked but had been ruffled through play, and her hair was in ponytail, but she still had bangs and little pieces of hair in her face. She looked at me with distrust. I knelt down to look her in the eyes, "I'm sorry nobody protected you. I am here now, and you do not have to be afraid. Stand behind me, no one will hurt you anymore." She was still hesitant, but she walked behind me, never losing her look of distrust.

I reached in and put my hand on the shoulder of a teenage me, dressed in baggy black pants and an expressionless face. She accepted my invitation to step out and I put my hands on her fresh wounds. "No more. You have suffered enough pain. You do not need to cause yourself more. You deserve love and I love you." I hugged her close and motioned for her to join her younger self.

Another teenage me looked out from the darkness, face bruised and swollen. I held my hand out palm up and offered her assistance stepping out. I put my hands on either side of her face and gently wiped away her tears. "I see you. You are marvelous and you matter. I am sorry no one has told you that before. And I am sorry no one else seems to care that you are hurt. I care, and I won't let anyone lay a hand on you again." She tried to smile, but it looked more like a grimace, as she stepped behind me.

A young adult me stood there, as a line of similar looking but differently dressed mes gathered to join her. I spoke to them as a group. "I'm sorry that nobody respected our boundaries and that fear always won our battles. I am sorry that no one listened when we tried to speak up. I will not let that happen again. Our boundaries are firm, and we know who we can trust now. Our voice is strong, and you are safe." As they stepped out of the shadow, they formed into one and joined those that came before them.

I looked back in. The next few did not see me, they were looking in their own personal mirrors, pulling at their skin and fixing their pose. Flexing and adjusting with sadness all over their faces. I reached in and pushed over each mirror one by one. As each mirror shattered, they looked at me with horror. My elementary self-wrapped her arms in front of her stomach, my adolescent self-covered her thighs, and my young adult self-tried to hide her protruding bones. My adult self just looked ashamed because there was too much of her to try to hide. I could see them. I could see their insecurity. I lifted my shirt slightly and pinched the fat on my stomach, put my hands on my thighs and jiggled them a bit. "It's okay, our bodies are supposed to do this. We are supposed to grow and change and move. It is part of being alive. And we can do so much with our body." I showed them pictures of rock climbing, skydiving, and aerial hoop. I showed them how much weight we can lift and the people around us cheering us on, because they do not even notice the cellulite or how our tummy folds over when we pick up the bar. "I'm sorry no one taught you that you are more than what you look like. That your worth was never found in your body. You are smart, capable, and beautiful!" The elementary aged one stepped forward and as she stepped out, the others vanished.

As I turned around once more, I saw the monster was much smaller now, only one left. As I faced the monster, it was like I was looking in the mirror. This was a reflection of my current self, the part of me that was still scared and scarred. She looked at me for help. "I'm still scared but I don't know why," she said to me. I grabbed her hands and looked her in the eye, "It's okay to be scared, but we know what we're doing now. You are beautiful, intelligent, and compassionate. You are an exquisite human being. You pour love into the world on a daily basis, but you deserve to love yourself too. And you are worthy of love! You are brave and bold. You are a masterpiece, and it is a privilege to know you. I am proud of how far you've come." Tears welled up in her eyes, she dropped my hands and wrapped her arms around my neck to hug me and the shadow around her began to fade. As she released me from our embrace, she looked at all of us and asked, "What now?" I nodded to invite her to join the group.

They huddled together and were talking amongst themselves, as I took a breath to speak, silence fell over them and they looked my way. "We have been through a lot. We have fought different battles on multiple fronts for as long as we can remember, but it is time to end this war. We have allowed the words and actions of others to drive us into fear and shame, but it was not our fault. We were supposed to be protected, we were supposed to be educated, we were supposed to be supported, we were supposed to be seen, we were supposed to be heard, and we were not. So, we learned how to survive. We do not want to just survive anymore, we want a bright and glorious life, because that is what we deserve. You are all the reason I am still standing today. You have kept this heart beating and these feet marching forward, no matter the foe we faced. It is my turn to take care of you. Let me."

I lined them up one by one, starting with the youngest, "You are brave and bold. Thank you for surviving, you can rest now." I kissed her on the forehead and hugged her as she became one with me.

Her baggy pants swooshed together as she stepped up to meet me, the fresh wounds she had just moments ago, had healed over and were scarring. "You are loved. Thank you for surviving, you can rest now." I kissed her forehead and again, we became one.

What was once a swollen face had healed and her grimace resembled a smile. "I see you; you are magnificent. Thank you for surviving, you can rest now." I kissed her forehead.

I approached the next, their long golden blonde hair hung over their shoulders, they looked impenetrable. "You have been strong. I hear you. Thank you for surviving," I put one hand on each shoulder, "You can rest now." As I kissed her on her forehead, she began to cry then melted into me.

I was looking at the childlike version of myself, same size and stature, but the face of a child. "You are beautiful and strong, just as you are. You have magic in your bones. I know this fight will still be hard, but we have got this. Thank you for surviving, you can rest now." She jumped at me and engulfed me in a hug, squeezing every firm and squishy part of me. She kissed me on the forehead and looked me in the eyes and with a determined gaze we joined.

At last, it was just me, and me. "This won't always be easy, but I need you to trust me. I need you to tell me when they are feeling hurt or scared so I can reassure them. But I need you to let them rest. They deserve rest." She nodded. "And I need you to remember. You are loved. You deserve love. Not everyone is able to give us the love we need. That does not make us unworthy or unlovable, it just means we must be able to love ourselves, even when no one else does. Can you do that for me?"

She nodded again. "You are a beautiful inspiration and my hero!"

"Of course, I am, I'm you."

Her eyes lit up and she smiled as I said at last, "Thank you for surviving, you can rest now."

I Understand

When I was young, I thought that I was all alone. Nobody knew how I felt, because nobody else had been through the same shit as me. I was alone in my pain. Luckily for me and unfortunately for the world around me, I was wrong. As I grew, I realized more and more that people shared the same stories as me. The same pain as me. And in realizing that I was not alone, I found a way to heal. And a new pain grew. A pain in knowing there are too many people who have been through the same shit I have. Too many people who have yet to discover that they are not alone. So now, I share my stories, for those who feel like they are the only ones, who feel like no one understands.

I understand.
I understand and you are not alone.
You are not alone and there is life on the other side of your pain.
There is life on the other side of your pain, and it is beautiful.
It is beautiful and healing is possible.
Healing is possible and it starts now.
It starts now.

C. S. Phoenix is a certified life coach, athletic trainer, and proud single mother of two. A BIPOC and LGBTQI+ ally, Phoenix is a strong advocate of open communication, empathy, and regaining power through vulnerability. When she isn't working or writing, Phoenix enjoys gardening, driving through the mountains, and playing a variety of sports. In the future, she hopes to travel to every continent and continue to bring courage to others by opening up about her own experiences.

CommonHumanityTWR.com

@C.S.Phoenix

Illustrator
Rachel Ross

Rachel is a multimedia artist with works in clay, acrylic paint, watercolor, ink, and other water-based mediums. She is an avid dog lover and water-skiing enthusiast. When she is not working, she is creating art, camping, or reading fantasy novels.

@rachelross87

Start Writing Your Story

Lightning Source UK Ltd.
Milton Keynes UK
UKHW030638100222
398427UK00004B/375